loud is
<u>not</u> a
language

Produced in Partnership with *Tall Pine Books*
119 E Center Street, Suite B4A | Warsaw, Indiana 46580
www.tallpinebooks.com

Paperback ISBN: 978-1-955546-37-9
Hardcover ISBN: 978-1-955546-38-6

| 1 22 22 20 16 02 |

Published in the United States of America

loud is
not a
language

Blueprints *for* Building Healthy
and Effective Communication

BRENDA COX HARKINS

THE LINAL® SERIES VOLUME 1

"I love this game changing book written for people that want to strengthen relationships and diffuse conflict by strategically valuing others' differences and listening with intention.

It's called *Loud Is Not A Language* or LINAL, for short.

The wisdom in this book gives clarity to step into conversations with conflict potential and diffuse it before it ever starts.

Brenda shows how to create powerful ways to have lasting influence and bring relationships into authentic understanding that does not require agreement.

She helps you build a roadmap to the why behind your own feelings and behaviors so that your awareness can keep your relationships healthy. And she reminds us that the best way to get people to care to understand our positions is to show them we care to understand theirs.

Brenda is a thought leader for today and I know that *Loud Is Not A Language* has the power to change an entire culture!"

—JENNIFER SCHRAMM
Entrepreneur

"Brenda has an amazing gift for looking at life with a unique perspective. "Loud is Not a Language" is an outstanding book that will make a huge difference in the market place."

—Michael McIntyre
Co-Founder, *Next Level Experience & McIntyre Business Accelerator*

"This book is both a challenging and profound message that is critical to any collaborative endeavor whether in the board room, church community or especially family relationships. I'm deeply provoked and convicted. Thank you for making it practical and understandable for all readers."

—Dr. Kim Vastine
Speaker, Author, Chaplain, and International Ambassador

"Brenda Cox Harkins has written a must-read for anyone who aims for clear communication that leads to relational capital, both in business and in personal relationships. *Loud Is Not A Language* will guide you through a journey in which you will be invited and challenged to push through racial, cultural and philosophical divides that are ever prevalent in our culture today. Not only will you be inspired, but you will also be instructed with practical steps towards positive change."

—Rob Moga
Operations Professional

This book is dedicated to my family. For loving me at my best, my worst, and in the many battles to tame my loud while still staying authentic, I am forever grateful. I love you all more than any words on a page could ever express.

CONTENTS

Foreword.. *II*

Introduction: This is Your Invitation...*13*

PART ONE: WHAT IT IS

1. Dinner Lessons *17*

2. The Meaning of "Loud" 27

3. Discovering a Different Way....................... 33

4. Pull Up a Chair...*41*

5. Deconstructing Loud.....................................*49*

PART TWO: HOW IT WORKS

6. L is for Listen *57*

7. O is for Own *69*

8. U is for Understanding 87

9. D is for Develop *99*

PART THREE: WHERE DO WE GO FROM HERE?

10. Reflection Exercises *107*

Part One Reflections...*109*

Part Two Reflections..*II2*

Relationship Check...*II5*

Chair Check...*II8*

Jump In *I23*

Author Bio *I27*

Acknowledgements..*I28*

Foreword

BRENDA HARKINS HAS an amazing gift for looking at life with a unique perspective. Loud Is Not A Language is an outstanding book that will make a huge difference in the market place.

We live in a time where our world has gone half crazy. Besides all the complex issues of our day that make communication a challenge, people have lost their ability to communicate over even the simplest things. Differences of opinions create enemies. It shouldn't be this way.

Brenda Harkins has discovered *more* than a better way to communicate. She has created a thought framework that begins with challenging the way we think about ourselves and others. This framework builds honor into our thought processes and allows people on different sides of various issues to experience respect from one other and build trust despite differences.

This thought framework shifts our focus from external issues to internal character. It challenges us to separate the two. To lay aside a person's particular stance on an issue for the purpose of understanding their character. That goes against the grain of our cancel culture and paves a way for people to walk in understanding of one another. As Brenda points out, understanding doesn't have to equal agreement.

Loud Is Not A Language is for anyone who values people and wants to understand how we can communicate beyond our differences. It explains in simple terms how to be more effective in our communication, how to build more fulfilling relationships, and how to have greater impact in how and whom we influence.

Loud Is Not A Language is also for anyone brave enough to honestly examine their own heart, their own motives, and their own judgments. It is for those who are willing to lay down their pride and ego for the purpose of gaining understanding around unfamiliar perspectives.

The Loud Is Not A Language thought framework honors people, their life journeys, their unique experiences, and the collaboration needed to harvest the treasure from those combined experiences. It also delivers a simple step-by-step process to begin incorporating this framework into all areas of society, from your homes to the marketplace.

Loud Is Not A Language has the potential to change our culture.

—MICHAEL MCINTYRE, *Next Level Experience*

This is Your Invitation

L OUD IS NOT A Language is not just a book. It is an invitation. I want to invite you to a new way of thinking. A way that honors the unique creation of each person and prioritizes understanding and love over correction.

This is not an invitation to compromise your values. It is an invitation to understand the values of others and why they have them.

This is an invitation to recognize every person on the planet has lived different experiences than you, and those experiences combined with their perspectives of those experiences, their core beliefs, their hurts, their hopes, and their personality make for an individual like no other. Each one of us is an individual like no other. Loud is Not a Language invites you to celebrate that and discover new ways to navigate relationships through that in a way that is both honoring and authentic to yourself and others.

This is an invitation to consider a way of thinking which has at its core the conviction that when we value one another despite our differences, we create powerful ways to have a lasting influence that makes a difference.

I invite you to explore this way of thinking.

I invite you to greater joy in your relationships.

I invite you to greater impact on your influence.

With great hope,

Brenda Harkins

PART ONE
WHAT IT IS

Part One is designed to help you understand what Loud Is Not A Language® (LINAL®) is all about. It explains what it is, what it isn't, and introduces the framework and process for communicating so that everyone can be heard.

LINAL® is a different way of communicating. One that breaks down walls and builds bridges. A way that respects others and builds relationships based on trust, all while increasing the effectiveness of our communication and influence even among people with differing ideas.

Influence without manipulation.

Doesn't that sound beautiful?

1
DINNER LESSONS

AT A SOCIAL dinner in 2016, I had an eye-opening encounter that drove home to me just how divided our world is, and how ineffective we are in our attempts to bridge the chasm.

My husband, Mike, and I met a friend for dinner at a city club where we sometimes attend business meetings, luncheons, or speaker events. This night was different. It was to be purely social, and we were looking forward to an enjoyable, relaxing evening. When we arrived, our friend was talking to a woman we had not met before. After being introduced, we realized she was there alone, so we invited her to join us for dinner. Then others arrived whom our new acquaintance knew, and it went from an intimate dinner to a lively gathering quickly, as our table continued to grow. Soon there were ten of us.

Most of us didn't know each other well. We had either just met or knew each other through business somehow. Bankers, business owners, and other professionals were at the table, and I mention that only because of my wrong assumption that intelligence equals emotional awareness. Knowing people mainly do business with those they know, like, and trust, I prioritize learning and genuinely caring about people, their views, and their interests, even when they differ from mine. I also make a point to be present, compassionate, and curious in our conversations. I know many wonderful people who do the same, so I guess I assumed that's how most people rolled. So much for assumptions.

The timing of this dinner was just weeks before the Clinton/Trump election and some brilliant soul decided it would be a good idea to turn the conversation political by asking...*So, what do you think about having the first woman president?*

The circus began. I remember sitting back in my chair observing the increasing tension and volume with surprise as each person, with their own set of convictions, tried passionately to convert the other person to their way of thinking. Some people were cheering for Clinton, while others praised

Trump. The Clintonites were in disbelief that "educated people could ever support" Trump, and the Trump tribe expressed the same sentiments back toward the Clinton crowd. Accusations of all sorts were flying on both sides. It would have been comedic if it hadn't been so mind-boggling. Two people got up and left the table without a word. It was that uncomfortable.

The dam burst when one of the people stood up and addressed a person at the other end of the table saying, *You don't actually believe that, do you?*

I still wonder...did they really think passion, insult, and accusation would influence a change of mind? Those tactics don't convince anyone.

Mike and I were seated near the middle of the table, and I felt like I was watching a tennis match. *Next volley!* I looked back and forth as they vied for points, each side trying to out-speak the other. Some with words, others with attitude, and in the midst of the chaos, it was like God leaned over the balcony of heaven and whispered this thought in my ear:

Loud is not a language.

I had never heard that phrase before. I had to think about it. Getting quiet, pondering, then looking back at seemingly intelligent people acting anything but, I got it. I understood. You see, loud is how you build barriers, not connections. Loud doesn't share thoughts, it screams them. It doesn't listen, it berates. Loud is how you end up being the only one left at the table when everyone else has walked away, which is what eventually happened.

Since that dinner, my passion and vision have increased more than ever to help people discover how to build respectful connections that foster trust, despite differences. Learning to utilize those differences can be an incredible advantage to exploring broader possibilities.

That dinner changed my world. The lessons I learned are invaluable. The understanding I received about the Loud is Not a Language® framework of communication has impacted every area of my life. It built bridges between different perspectives throughout the Covid pandemic and racial tensions of 2020 and beyond, reaching families and businesses and relationships that were strained in a whole new way.

I want to share the three main lessons I learned from that evening in hopes that they will have a positive impact on you, just like they did me.

LESSON 1: IF WE WANT TO BE UNDERSTOOD, WE MUST LISTEN TO UNDERSTAND.

Everyone voicing their opinions that night wanted to be heard and understood. Each one felt passionately, for their own personal reasons, about the candidates and their stance on various issues. They believed what they believed so strongly that they got forceful in trying to make others believe the same way.

We do that, don't we?

If we don't walk away, which has no influence either, we tend to get overly zealous. That is not the way to attract an understanding audience unless they already agree with you, then there is no need for influence.

It's counterintuitive, but the best way to be heard, and potentially understood, is to listen. The best way to get people to even *care* to understand our positions is to show them we care to understand theirs.

Nobody was understood that night. And if anyone was heard it was because the volume and attitude were unavoidable. I guarantee it wasn't because the words penetrated. The only influence that night was a negative influence. People walked away more sold on their ideas than ever, and more convinced that "the other side" was crazy. Because they were. Both sides. Crazier than any adults I have ever experienced, at least within a professional sphere.

We must listen to understand if we hope to have others understand us.

LESSON 2: IF WE CHANGE NOTHING, NOTHING CHANGES.

That seems obvious, doesn't it? If we don't change anything, we won't see any change! Yet our behavior often shows differently. When we want something to change, we tend to resist any thoughts or actions that would change us. We want change to happen out there, among "them", not personally within us. We talk more about the same thing, louder about the same thing, and hope to widen the circle we consider "our side." Nothing really changes. It's kind of like that definition that says insanity is doing or saying the same thing over and over but expecting different results.

Thinking about this logically we know it doesn't make sense, but when we are caught up in the passion and emotion of a certain issue, we don't think logically. We think emotionally.

When was the last time you felt strongly about something, but others didn't agree? What did you do? Get louder? Shrink back? Those attitudes are on display either way. Neither behavior influences with positive impact. It may manipulate. It may allow you to get your way at the moment. But the change won't be lasting. Unfortunately, the resentment felt by others, once they realize they were manipulated, might.

Learning to pay attention to our emotions takes discipline. Consistent discipline. Once learned, that discipline enables us to utilize our emotions for real change. Change that will make a difference. Even negative emotions can positively trigger us. They can remind us to pause, breathe, think, or pray before taking the next step. This helps ensure the next step is thought out and wise. Stepping *wisely* into a conversation with conflict potential can diffuse the conflict before it ever gets started.

How do we do this? How do we learn to pay attention to our emotions? How do we allow even negative emotions to move us forward? We must change some things. Change some of our ways. Change some of our thinking. Change some of our mindsets.

In the next chapter, we will delve more deeply into *how* to make these changes. But be assured, if we change nothing, nothing changes. If we are not willing to change anything, we might as well stop hoping others will change. Courage to take bold steps toward what is possible, and humility to lay down our ego, are both needed to make the changes necessary for this type of growth environment. Those two qualities, courage and humility, create endless opportunities for fruitful relationships. The impossible possibilities are endless.

LESSON 3: RESPECT BUILDS BRIDGES. DISRESPECT BUILDS WALLS.

Since 2020 there have been some seriously rocky times with someone very dear to me. Their views are about as far from mine as Texas Chili is from Tofu. And vice versa. But I am not willing to let a difference of perspectives destroy a treasured relationship with a person I love. I am grateful they feel the same toward me.

We have had many tears together over some of the issues that could divide us, but the bottom line is that we are both committed to respecting the right for each of us to hold our own views. We don't even respect each other's views. We just respect 1) each other, and 2) the right for each of us to have our own views. That has gotten us over some mountains of fear, anger, and heartbreak that threatened damage to our relationship.

Whether it's a relationship dear to you, or a relationship you just hope to influence, respect is the bridge that will walk you over the relational canyon to the other side. Without that bridge, you could easily lose sight of the potential waiting on the other side. Respect establishes trust between opposing canyon walls.

What does respect *look like* in hard conversations?

When there is tension and conflict, respect

looks like valuing another person's individuality and right to think for themselves. We don't have to like their opinions. We just need to respect their right to have them. After all, if God does that for us, shouldn't we do it for each other?

Respect builds trust. With trust, enemies can become allies. Without trust, even your allies can become enemies.

This is hard stuff. I am not suggesting it is easy. But we can do hard things.

Questions are a great way to step into hard conversations. The right questions that show genuine interest in understanding another's views, or understanding the reasons for the views they hold, is an open invitation for their views to be heard and understood. When people feel heard and understood, they also feel respected, and respect is almost always reciprocal.

Reciprocity means you get an opportunity to be heard and understood by them as well, and when you hear and understand one another, even if you still disagree, there is potential for growth and positive change. Because you now trust and accept one another with your differences.

One of the biggest reasons people resist change is their lack of conviction that change is needed. If our sincere respect can build trust bridges to their side of the canyon, then that bridge can open our hearts and theirs to hear and at least try to understand our separate convictions.

Some of the best friends I have had throughout my life have held differing views on topics I held dear. But they were also friends that didn't base relationship on uniformity. Our trust in one another was greater. I am grateful for those relationships. They have helped me gain the courage to build more bridges.

2

The Meaning of "Loud"

PEOPLE ASK WHAT "loud" means because there are obviously times when volume is necessary. Loud is partially volume, but not only volume. Loud is also an attitude that creates emotionally unsafe environments for sharing differences of opinion. It can express itself overtly with aggression, and sometimes arrogance, or covertly as perhaps passive aggression which is *felt* as emotionally loud. Loud builds walls that keep others out. Loud is verbal, emotional, and sometimes physical. People default to loud when they emphatically believe they are right, want to protect themselves, and are determined to have the upper hand.

Language is designed for people to communicate. At the core, language allows conversations to be reciprocal. If you speak only English, you will not be able to communicate well with someone who speaks only Spanish, Mandarin, Hindi, or Swahili. Your conversations cannot be reciprocal. Even though hand gestures, facial expressions, and body language also communicate, without the right verbal language, the best we can hope for is that our assumptions, and theirs, are right about what we are communicating. Loud is not a language because it is not reciprocal. Loud has no interest in understanding another perspective. People who speak loud aren't interested in reciprocity. Thus, the title: *Loud Is Not A Language*®.

Loud is Not a Language® (aka **LINAL**®) is a simple thought framework for higher quality communication, relationship, and influence. It is not a mind-blowing philosophy. It is a simple, practical, and doable process for anyone willing to back up from their own narrative long enough to hear and care about the narratives of people whose life experiences have been very different. No agreement is necessary. Just genuine care and compassion.

That said, preparation for using the process isn't always easy. It can be uncomfortable at times. A humble heart is needed. One that is willing to search out some things that may be hidden under the surface; things that don't serve anybody well.

Seeing those blind spots takes courage and a willingness to grow. Unfortunately, growth and comfort don't coexist.

The focus of LINAL® is on honoring people, even in their differences, and creating emotionally safe environments for producing dynamic, constructive, and advantageous relationships. These types of relationships create space to discover great solutions for the problems we face today.

Emotionally safe environments are created when we honor people. Think about that. When someone genuinely honors us with their actions or words, there is a bond that develops, creating an atmosphere of safety. LINAL® brings honor into every conversation. In this crazy world we live in, with more problems popping up every day, the safety of honoring environments also helps with collaboration. It stirs up creativity to develop much-needed solutions.

Because collaboration increases communication, we learn from each other's stories, skills, and experiences. Collaboration invites engagement from everyone. The end results of these brainstorming and joint efforts are often positive innovations and higher energy for continued productivity.

LINAL® first looks at the environment needed for an important conversation to take place before focusing on the solutions needed. Emotionally safe environments are accepting, curious, and compassionate. We can focus on the problem or the needed solutions all day long, but we won't get the creativity and flow of ideas needed if a safe environment hasn't been created first. The LINAL® process helps people understand how to do this. Providing safety opens doors for people to share a wide array of ideas. Innovation comes with consideration and openness to new ways of thinking.

Creativity thrives where people are accepted and their ideas are openly considered. In unsafe environments where people are concerned about ridicule or rejection, creativity is stifled. People hold back and are more hesitant to share. It's as if a clamp was placed on their free-flowing ideas and now the pipeline is clogged. Freedom to be creative, and to express new and even crazy ideas, is what produces dynamic, constructive, and gratifying solutions. A big bonus is that relationships are strengthened in that environment as well.

LINAL® encourages honest inspection of your environment. What conditions and influences surround you personally? What about your family? Your team? Your organization?

What surrounds us is important. Providing an externally welcoming environment makes a difference in people accepting us, our words, and our ideas, or not. Do we provide a welcoming environment?

What emanates from us is equally or more important. That would be the atmosphere we live from. So, it's not just our environment that opens people up or shuts them down, it is the atmosphere of our environment. The feeling they get when they are in our environment.

What do people feel when they are in our environment? Paying attention to how they act, how they interact, and what they say helps us easily pick up on their comfort, or discomfort, levels. Whether it is with you, your family, or your workplace, their behaviors will give insight you wouldn't see otherwise because your environment feels normal to you.

Acceptance and encouragement are at the top of the list for providing space to create great solutions. Do your surroundings inspire the sharing of ideas? Do you encourage it? Do people feel their contributions will be appreciated and considered?

If so, congratulations! You have an environment and an atmosphere that is ripe for planting the seeds of Loud Is Not A Language®.

3

DISCOVERING A DIFFERENT WAY

I T'S NO SECRET that our world is more divided than ever before.

Opinions abound. Opposing opinions abound. And *everyone* thinks *they* are right.

Our landscape is full of fear, anxiety, and uncertainty. What we do not understand, what is foreign to our normal, is what we often attack. Since 2020 we have seen that truth on steroids.

Fast forward to 2023 and there were three major bank closures in the month of March alone, two of which are the second and third-largest bank failures in the history of our country. Things are shaky, to say the least. Fear underlies much of the news, as well as much of our thinking.

The predictable thing about fear is that it will either shrink back or attack what it believes created it. Anger is often a resulting behavior of fear. But since it's not possible to directly attack the 264 tornadoes in the past three months, or the collapsing financial situations, or the war in Ukraine, or the pharmaceutical industry, or the death of a loved one, or whatever big issues keep us awake at night... instead, we attack one another for actions and beliefs that differ from ours, placing blame on those people, believing their beliefs or actions were the cause.

Covid speaks to this, too. Since we can't just take down a virus, we fear Covid because there has been tragic suffering and loss from it, and we don't know where it will hit next. I am going to risk stepping on some toes here, but just softly. Please don't get hung up on this example; it is just extremely relevant to this time we are living in.

It's likely we either believe vaccines are part of the solution or we believe they are part of the problem. Whichever way you believe, it is probably safe to assume there are some not-so-pleasant feelings toward those who disagree. You may argue that their stance shows ignorance and that applying some wisdom (your wisdom) could help stop this virus. But even underneath that, the passion to stop it has an element of fear, and fear causes people to either shrink back or attack whatever stirs it up. Most often, that fear is directed toward those who believe differently, linking them personally to the problem. So where do we go from here?

Imagine what could happen if we hit pause on all our panic buttons long enough to learn a different way. Learning and applying that way to one issue and seeing the powerful impact it has to promote change, encourages us to then apply it to the next issue that arises. And the next, and the next, and the next. Soon a new way, a different way, becomes normal. That is my hope for Loud Is Not A Language®. May it be a different way that promotes positive change.

That is the purpose of this book. To learn a different way that makes a positive difference. To learn a way that does more than fight and yell and point fingers. Because let's be real. Has anyone ever positively influenced you by focusing on how wrong you are? Most likely not. And you won't influence others, at least not in a lasting way, by focusing on how wrong they are either. But I do believe it is possible, even with different perspectives, to truly see people, hear their concerns, and learn to validate even what doesn't resonate—if for no other reason than knowing those concerns hold as much value to them as yours hold to you.

We are all in this crazy mixed-up world together, doing the best we can with what we know, and when we value other people right where they are and extend love and honor, things can change. Honor. Respect. Building trust. Being a safe place for others emotionally, spiritually, and relationally. Imagine what might happen if we chose to intentionally live out of those ways more, and spread it around.

It is my desire to help our world understand this is possible.

I can't think of any area in our society that doesn't need to communicate better, to build better relationships, to show up with respect, and to influence without manipulation.

Picture all that could be different if...

- Children learned, at an early age, how to listen and try to understand others and value their perspectives even when they disagree.
- Parents built bridges of faith, confidence, and trust with their children— bridges that reach their teens during the hard years when there is often experimentation with ideas and behaviors that go against what is best for them.
- Business and nonprofit leaders gave their

people permission to develop their unique strengths and appreciate the different strengths of others while allowing them to fail and learn and grow. Instead of playing it safe and delivering mediocre results, they were encouraged to risk going all-in on the challenges set before them.

- Pastors and people of faith taught *and were taught* how to reach out with love to people with differing values instead of judging, criticizing, and condemning them without ever compromising their own values.

- Expected behaviors—whether at home, office, church, or in public—stopped being driven by fear, anxiety, and skepticism and switched to a growth mindset based on faith, courage, love, and action.

My hope is that the journey through these pages will awaken an awareness of how important it is to see *inside ourselves* so that we can then see *beyond ourselves*. When we honestly and courageously look first at what is *in* us, we can then deal with whatever is needed to see *beyond* us. Whether an adjustment in perspective, healing of a heart wound, forgiveness for something that has embittered us, or a number of other possibilities, this awareness is needed for our pure and real influence to do its powerful work. My hope is that it will awaken a good dose of both compassion and wisdom, as well as an understanding of how our thoughts, feelings, and behaviors—even subconsciously—affect others. *Because we sometimes work against the very things we want the most.*

Loud is Not a Language® is a quest to communicate with respectful understanding toward other people and their differences, build trusting relationships, influence without manipulation, and teach how to truly love people right where they are. If you are a people leader, and everyone from parents to presidents are, *then **lead** people.* Don't railroad them. Go before them, go with them, show them the way, influence them wisely, and guide them without manipulating the outcome. Loud is Not a Language® can help you do that.

This method is built on respect, which is why the pause button must be activated. Nobody hits pause when fear and anger are in the driver's seat, and respect isn't built by those companions, either. When you hit pause and give respect a try, you can see the rapport that builds. Greater quality relationships and influence without manipulation will result. This method requires courageous, compassionate authenticity, and when people utilize this method *with respect for that authenticity,* it creates environments where there is no need for anyone to compromise their values, ever.

- Loud is an attitude as much as it is volume.
- Loud is an opinion, not conversation.
- Loud pushes people away from the very thing to which we want to draw them.
- Loud shuts down the listening part of language.
- Loud cannot coexist with love.

Let me be clear. I have messed up more than my fair share of times by being too loud about my passions and convictions. By being driven by fear. I have met numerous people who make the same mistakes, especially those that embrace strong ideals. We think being loud about what is loud in our hearts will persuade others to see it our way, but the opposite is most often the case. We send people running in the other direction.

I think of the adage...*people don't care how much you know unless they know how much you care.* Why would we care what someone who strongly disagrees with our convictions has to say? Unless we know that person cares about us and is speaking to us from a place of genuine love and concern. We might listen then.

Old habits die hard and communicating differently doesn't come easy. An internal shift is needed. Convictions, values, and beliefs can be very loud. A shift in mindset, the learning of a new way, over time, can quiet the noise. Even the noise within.

If we want what's loud inside us to be heard, we must break loud down into bite-size pieces for others to chew on. The LINAL® process I will share with you in this book is designed to help you do just that.

I invite you to join me in the discovery of more impactful, authentic, compassionate ways to influence positive relationships with others. The kind that builds trust and can make a lasting difference.

4

PULL UP A CHAIR

I LOVE ACROSTICS. They help me remember things. There are two important ones in this book that can help us remember how to shift our ways of communicating. CHAIR is the first one. It is a prerequisite to effectively utilizing the LINAL® framework (which will reveal the second acrostic in the next chapter).

CHAIR helps us establish the right heart motives for having constructive conversations which are possible. Sit back, get gut honest with yourself, and make any adjustments needed to sit *comfortably* in this CHAIR. The LINAL® framework is just another formula without the CHAIR qualities present. However, with them, the framework is transformational.

You have probably heard the expression, "Pull up a chair." This is used when a person is asked to join a conversation. It is the welcoming attitude needed to hear new ideas. It is inviting others into a conversation so that *they* can be heard. Now that is a different way of communicating. At least for most of us. Our default tends to invite others to a conversation so that *we* can be heard. This is the start of a new way. Pull up a CHAIR and invite others to be heard.

What is the CHAIR?

<u>C</u>ourage.

<u>H</u>umility.

<u>A</u>uthenticity.

<u>I</u>ntegrity.

<u>R</u>espect.

These five characteristics make the power of your impact possible. For it to be effective, though, each of these characteristics must be genuine. That requires looking at whoever is across from you with these five values absolutely settled in your mind, soul, and spirit. With that dedication, you can make a difference in the lives of people you never dreamed of.

COURAGE
(to step into the hard conversations)

It takes COURAGE to step into hard conversations.

Remember that courage is the conviction that something is more important than your fear. So, imagine the best possible outcome for the conversation you think needs to be had. The conversation you aren't excited about having. The one that could go south quickly. Imagine the best possible outcome. Now, is that outcome more important than your fear? Would it be worth pressing through the fear to attempt to achieve it? If so, you have found your key to courage. Step into those hard, but needed conversations with a focus on what is more important than the fear.

HUMILITY
(to not think better of yourself than you do of others)

Humility is to think of others, their opinions, their perspectives, their ideas, and their experiences as being just as important as your own. I have heard it said that humility is not thinking less of yourself but thinking of yourself less. When entering a hard conversation, that is certainly true. Have you ever tried discussing a conflict by letting the other person know why *your* opinion is so important? If so, my bet is that it didn't go too well. But when we can shift our focus to hearing and understanding *their* opinion, and

> "Courage is the conviction that something is more important than your fear."

making that the priority, we can get somewhere.
Humility is keeping yourself in check by remembering everyone has a story that comes with unique
perspectives because of their experiences, and
those stories are every bit as valuable as mine...or
yours. Humility helps us lean in to listen for those
things from others we may not have understood, or
cared to understand, before.

AUTHENTICITY
(to be real about who you are)

Authenticity requires being real about who we are.
Being honest. You care about who people think you
are. If we are honest, most of us do to some degree.
We care how we are seen by others. At the core, we
want to be seen for who we truly are and what we
truly represent. But in times when other people's
opinions may have a significant impact on the direction of our life or career, we may default to wanting to be seen for how they want us to be. Authenticity doesn't allow for that.

The *power* of our presence comes when people
think we are who we *really* are. When others think
we are something we are not, that will eventually disappoint. It's not sustainable to be somebody
else. The *impact* on how we show up is exponential-
ly greater when our outward persona aligns with
our internal reality. Hiding our weaknesses is like

playing make-believe. Vulnerabilities cause us to be relevant and relatable. Be authentic. Be vulnerable. It matters.

INTEGRITY
(to check your motives for whether they are trustworthy)

The key to operating with integrity is to check our motives and be certain they are trustworthy. Ask yourself WHY you are doing what you are doing.

- Why do I want to have this conversation?
- Why am I saying what I am saying?
- What is the motivator driving me?

Answer honestly. Nobody else is listening. Then ask yourself whether you would consider another person trustworthy if they operated with those same motives.

You may discover the reason you really wanted to have that conversation was so that you could convince them to see things your way. Hmmmm. There's more about this in Part Two, but when our motives are to convince someone to think our way, some say that borders on manipulative motives. I say it *is* a manipulative motive. Would you trust someone whom you knew the motive was to control the way you think? Would you consider them a person of integrity for setting up a conversation with you based on only a pretense that they cared? When their real motive was to shift you over to their way of thinking?

It's human desire to want people to agree with us. But to do things to specifically cause that is a fine line to walk. Hearing *their* heart, *their* thoughts, *their* ideas, and exploring more about why those things are important to *them* often causes reciprocity. However, beware of your motives. If the only reason you are listening is to get reciprocity, that motive meter is pointing south. If we don't care, genuinely care, about their perspectives, then the whole setup is selfishly motivated. That's ugly. At a minimum, it is *not* integrity.

Sometimes our desires deceive us. Doing a personal checkup, or check-in, can help shine a light on those desires, but it requires the courage to be honest. An honest look helps us identify any less-than-honest motives and prioritizes integrity so that we can make the adjustments needed. Internally and externally.

RESPECT
(to honor the different perspectives of others)

Honoring others, their perspectives, and their differences, is not only respectful but also persuasive. A word of caution here, much like the one above.

Showing respect to get what you want is called manipulation. That isn't pulling up a CHAIR. It is not courageous, humble, authentic, integrous, or respectful. To disguise manipulation as respect is a serious violation of trust. But when we honor others by listening with a true desire to understand, this can go a long way in bridging the gaps our misunderstandings and opposing views cause.

Respect others. It appreciates and shows consideration for them. Respect plays a big role in how others feel about themselves, and how secure they feel in their relationship with us. Respect matters. Let's sow more of those seeds.

Embracing these five "CHAIR" qualities, settling into each one, and being confident in them is essential for having hard but constructive conversations. When we grab hold of them and utilize them by honestly evaluating ourselves through them, we not only become more self-aware, we become more genuine and more compassionate toward the things that matter to others.

Becoming more aware of what motivates us enables us to make the necessary changes and corrections for being the best version of ourselves. We can then increase the quality of our relationships by genuinely caring for others, being real, and proving ourselves trustworthy. We all need more relationships like that in our lives. How great to *be* that relationship for others!

Embracing the CHAIR qualities can also increase the impact of your communication and influence. When you step in with courage and humility, being authentically you, operating with integrity, and showing genuine respect, what you say will land much more effectively than trying to convince someone you are right and they are wrong.

These qualities build stronger families, business teams, churches, and communities. They affect every area of our lives because they reflect what's internally genuine in our lives. More positive environments are created by embracing these five qualities. Even conflict takes on a new dynamic of being constructive vs. destructive.

How you show up in every relationship you have will determine, to a large extent, what that relationship develops into, or doesn't. Courage, humility, authenticity, integrity, and respect are hugely influential in the health of all our relationships.

5
DECONSTRUCTING LOUD

CONSTRUCTING AND DECONSTRUCTING. To construct something is to build it. To deconstruct is to break it down or dismantle it. We are either building or breaking down structures all the time. Most often in our minds. Even subconsciously. And often we don't even realize the structure is there until someone points it out to us. Think about it.

Let's say you were bitten by a dog as a young child. You might construct the belief that all dogs are mean and scary. Are all dogs mean and scary? Of course not. But your childhood experience didn't differentiate that. It just took the experience and generalized it. That's what we do unless we pay attention to the belief that is forming and deconstruct it before it is fully formed. Awareness and intentionality are required to do that. Two things most children don't even think about.

As we mature, we have a better understanding of how to identify and dismantle wrong beliefs, *if we are intentional*. Take needles, for example. Maybe you are terrified of getting a shot when you go to the doctor. Or getting blood taken. (That would be me.) I have memories of being held down by a doctor and nurse and them making my mom leave the room when I was a little girl because I started crying when they said I had to get a shot. I remember seeing the needle, feeling scared, the nurse semi-pushing my mom out of the room, her not wanting to leave, and me being held down. I am sure the shot didn't hurt like I remember it hurting, but I constructed a belief that day that shots are terrifying. The truth is what's terrifying is having your security removed when you are a frightened child and being physically controlled by someone you feel is going to hurt you. Logically, I know shots aren't terrifying. Emotionally, I don't. So, when I get blood taken, for example, I am intentional to be aware of the false construct and tell myself the truth. Every time I do, the false construct gets dismantled a little bit more. It's close to gone now, but not all the way. Every time *you* do that to whatever false constructs *you* have built, they get taken down a little more, as well.

So, what does that have to do with loud?

Loud is a construct. It was built for a reason. It may have been modeled, so it felt normal. But in whatever way it came to be built, it is a construct made for dealing with opposition or fear or not being in control, or just fill in the blank with whatever is personally uncomfortable. Once built, it defaults to being our normal.

What does it mean to deconstruct loud? It means we take it apart, piece by piece, by looking at the truth of how ineffective it is. The second acrostic I talked about is used in this dismantling by literally deconstructing the word "LOUD." Part Two goes into that process more deeply.

Think of the last time you were loud. It could have been with a negative attitude, a disrespectful tone, or increased volume. How did that work out for you? Did it work *for* what you wanted? Or did it work *against* it?

Pay attention to the times you are loud. Be aware of others' reactions to it. Feel the atmosphere of the conversation shift. Note the tension. Doing this and being intentional to act in a counter manner, will dismantle the loud structure one brick at a time.

Loud shuts down dissenting voices. You may be thinking, yes! That's what we want! Shut down the dissenting voices! People listen best when they know their voice counts, too. So, loud drives people away. It offends. If you want to truly be heard and not just talk, Loud must be deconstructed. If you want to be worthy of a respectful ear, show others they are worthy of yours.

You have probably heard of Legos®. You know, the little—and not so little—plastic shapes that connect with other shapes to build things? On their official Lego® YouTube channel, it states: *We hope to inspire and develop the builders of tomorrow...*
So do I. But why wait for tomorrow? I want to inspire and develop the builders of today, too, so that *they* can help influence the builders of tomorrow.

> "People listen best when they know their voice counts, too."

Putting words, actions, and volume together is much like putting those plastic pieces together. They build something. When we take care in putting them together, especially while sitting in the CHAIR, what we build can be recognized and understood. It can be impactful. Sometimes even amazing.

I know all too well what it looks like to put your

words together wrong. Or your attitude. Or your volume. I have learned a lot, not just from that dinner in 2016, but from my own life experience of being too loud and pushing away the very ones I wanted to draw near. I want to pass on to you the lessons I have learned in hopes that together we can inspire and develop the builders of today *and* tomorrow. We can help them construct and deconstruct well.

Trying to fit a small Lego® piece made for older children into a larger piece made for preschoolers doesn't work. The parts that connect are different sizes, so as much as you try, they will still be put together wrong. Loud is like that. It is simply put together wrong for having positive interactions. Interactions that matter. That make a difference. It doesn't work. Deconstructed, though, each letter has incredible value. Take a look. This second acrostic creates a strong, effective, trustworthy bridge for connecting various perspectives.

L: Listen to truly understand, not reply.

O: Own your journey and the biases that come with it.

U: Understand the biases of others due to their unique experiences.

D: Develop new ways to move forward.

Sounds simple, right? This will resonate more

as we dive deeper into each of the letters in the next four chapters. You will see the value that has walked people through racial tensions, covid restrictions, family discord, and so much more. With a desire to respectfully understand the *why* behind the differences, so much genuine understanding is possible. Perhaps not agreement, but understanding doesn't require agreement.

Let's go deeper! Pull up a CHAIR, and let's deconstruct LOUD.

See you in Part Two...

HOW IT WORKS

In Part One, you saw how the CHAIR was the *preparation* for this communication process. In Part Two, the *process* involved in the LINAL® framework is explained.

Here you will find practical steps to create inviting environments that are safe for having those hard conversations. The ones that are all too easy to avoid. Neglect doesn't bring change though, does it? Neglect allows wounds, imaginations, and resentment to grow even bigger.

This process is not easy. It is simple, though. They are not the same.

LINAL® is doable for those who have courageous hearts, a desire for change, and compassion for people. It will help you walk through what is needed so that you can grow in both your influence and your relationships.

6

L is for LISTEN

WE HAVE ALL been there. We are talking and someone, or multiple someones, interrupt us. They throw in a random comment or start a completely different train of thought, and soon we have lost ours. The train has left the station and the thoughts are gone. Distractions can do that.

We feel valued when others truly listen. When they want to understand what we say. We have a desire to be heard, and when that desire is met, when others pay attention to our thoughts and ideas, even asking questions to understand more fully, that makes us feel appreciated. Being heard feels good. But here is the big question: Are we willing to do the same for others?

People interrupt each other all the time. Have

you noticed? Maybe they think what they have to say is important enough to warrant interruption. Maybe they don't think at all. But it is entertaining to watch when it is not maddening. Next time you are in a group conversation, pay attention to this. You will see it everywhere.

Sometimes people want to tell us how what we said reminded them of something that happened to them back in whatever year with whatever person. Fascinating. Or they want to fact-check us, or give us advice, or let us know the same thing happened to them, or offer correction, or share their great wisdom, or whatever it is they think is worthy of hearing above what we are saying. OR...*maybe we are those someones*. Maybe we are the ones waiting, or not waiting, for a break in the conversation so that we can interrupt, chiming in with whatever flies into our brains. After all, we have something people need to hear, right? And right at that moment! Because God forbid *we* forget what we were going to say. I mean, it has to be said. And right now.

Interruptions not only distract the speaker, but they also send the message that we think what we have to say is more important than what they are saying. I can hear you now. *No! I don't think it's more important. I will just forget if I don't say it now... or...I didn't mean to interrupt, but...or...this is really im-*

portant, and I will be quick. Let's be honest. At some level, we do feel our input *is* more important or we wouldn't jump in to give it.

Feeling it doesn't make it true.

No matter how important we feel the information is, it is almost always more important to respect the person speaking. To give them our full attention by being present in the moment with them. In our world of quick information available literally at our fingertips, I fear our brains have been trained to value that information above the people right in front of us.

Information, thoughts, and ideas are all good and fun and interesting. But they come and go. Unless we are working on some big project where a missing piece of information is going to be the game changer, information is just more knowledge that can wait. There is a time for that. But it is not in the middle of someone sharing their thoughts with us. Giving space...being present...listening...that's the game changer.

This doesn't mean all conversations need to be serious. If you think that is what I am saying it is probably because listening seems like a lot of work to you. It's not listening that is the hard work, though. It is changing a habit that is the hard work. If you are in the habit of interrupting and not fully listening to understand, this is for you. Once you see the benefits of listening to understand, the rewards that come from allowing someone to be heard, you will change your perspective.

Conversation is an ebb and flow of thoughts and ideas between people. If only one person is talking, it is a monologue instead of a conversation. But sensitivity to timing, being aware of the right time to respond, is important. When we listen to understand, this timing flows naturally. We aren't waiting to jump in with our comments, and when we do respond, it is relevant. And timely. We may even ask questions to understand at a deeper level. Learning to listen for the purpose of understanding is an unexpected joy for those who haven't yet practiced it. It is an expected and anticipated joy for those who are already practiced.

> "Giving space... being present... listening... that's the game changer."

Before we go further, I do want to acknowledge that some conversations are more frivolous and fun than others. You know the ones! Where people chime in here and there, make jokes, laugh, play games, or just enjoy the fun of being together. When the conversation consists of lighthearted banter or things like...*Did you try that amazing cheese dip? Or, Who wants to get in the pool?* These are not the times we are focused so much on listening. However, there is never a *bad* time to listen.

Why do people talk? Because they want you to hear? Maybe. Probably. But more accurately, *they want to be heard.* It's a subtle difference, but a difference all the same. If they want *you* to hear, their focus is on you. If they want to be heard, their focus is on them. So, when we are thinking of that person's desire to be heard and let that desire take priority over our interjections, and when we really listen to understand what they want us to hear, we show respect. As the last step in the CHAIR preparation mentioned, respect builds trust. And trust is a foundation on which you can build just about anything.

Trust can be established in the simplest of conversations, just by sincerely listening to understand the point, the heart, or the suggestion. Once it is established, those harder conversations that inevitably come up will already have that strong foundation of trust, which makes going to the harder places easier and more productive. Operating from a base of trust is a great advantage at any time, especially when there is a need to resolve problems.

Hard conversations need to happen more often. Our world is full of loud monologues. When we master the art of listening to understand, we will have a rich contribution to conversations that can make a difference. It is in day-to-day listening to understand that trust is built. That's where it starts, and we have plenty of opportunities to practice.

Listening for the purpose of truly understanding, instead of convincing, is a beautiful thing. The flow of conversation is rich with ideas and creativity, and with listening to understand as the focus, patterns of interrupting or being interrupted fall away.

Sounds great, but how do we walk this out? When our whole world seems loud and unforgiving, how do we listen? How do we bend our ears to those that are unbending? And why?

With so many people operating from a place of high stress, fear, uncertainty, or anger, it is difficult to know how to step into those important conversations. It's even difficult knowing which conversations *are* important to step into! Some feel intimidating. Others feel useless. We are balancing between metaphorical red lights and caution lights constantly. Where have all the green lights gone?

Getting caught up in that kind of thinking stalls us out. We do nothing. Believing that the right thing to do is rarely nothing, several years ago I implemented a new way of thinking. Instead of sitting at those symbolic red lights waiting for them to turn green, I chose to see green lights unless I am shown red. I mean, if you are going to make a mistake, why not make it while trying to do something instead of nothing, right?

This thinking moved me out of my stuck place, and yes, I make plenty of mistakes. Do I learn? I sure do. And it teaches me more than sitting around doing nothing ever would. So green light it is! That is my game plan.

I apply that same thinking to listening now. I assume there is a green light to listen, understand, and ask clarifying questions if needed. It is obvious soon after entering the intersection if the light was red instead, and usually, some form of loudness informs me of that. That's okay. Red lights eventually turn green unless they are completely broken. So don't get too bummed by the red lights you encounter. Stay available. Stay sincere. Stay humble. If it changes, you will be ready.

For those green light conversations, I cannot overstate the importance of being genuine. If I am asking questions about their feelings, I need to care about their feelings. If I am asking questions about their position, I need to care about their position. Listening is for the purpose of understanding what they have to say. Otherwise, I am not in it to understand. I am just asking questions for the sole purpose of hoping they will listen to me. And that sole purpose is a terrible soul purpose. It is called manipulation, and manipulation is counterfeit caring.

Genuine caring listens to the perspectives of others even when they differ from our own. That is not always easy. When our convictions are opposed, how do we care? Why do we care? When beliefs, perspectives, or opinions oppose our own and our fight mode turns on, it usually doesn't even register to most of us the need to care. And honestly, it's not so much the views we should care about. It is the people who hold them. Those are often hard to separate, though, so genuine caring requires at least *understanding* their views.

So how do we care?

Why do we care?

Those are legitimate questions.

In an attempt to answer them, it is important to realize that people's perspectives are not our enemies. They are just their perspectives. They are subject to change, as are ours as much as we may hate to admit that. Perspectives are held because of life experiences. Different life experiences can shift those perspectives. Take the time to pause, breathe, and remember the views of others are only that. Views. This gives us the opportunity to lay down our weapons, which are often our words, tones, and attitudes. It allows us to utilize peace even among our differences.

Utilize peace. What does that mean?

I have seen over and over that even when others think *our* views are *their* enemy, when we operate in peace and ask questions from a place of peace, that peace becomes an act of war on the confusion and lies that pit us against each other. And conversations happen. Things change. Relationships are built. Trust is developed. Curiosity is deepened. And ultimately, that peace makes a way for influence that is not manipulation. Because the goal isn't agreement. The goal is understanding.

Understanding is a powerful relationship builder that keeps doors open for future conversations. Discerning and taking note of what is *in us*, such as what we believe and why, makes a way for us to deal wisely with what is *beyond us,* which is what others believe and why.

When we listen to understand others, we don't always influence the *way* we would like, but we influence. We may want to influence someone to support a certain political candidate that we support, much like the people at the dinner party back in 2016. But when you listen to understand their perspectives, and why they believe as they do, the influence that may actually happen could look like them having a change of mind that all (fill in your last party of choice) are not evil, unreasonable, stupid, or whatever they might have thought prior to you taking the time to listen to understand. Is that influence? It sure is! Might that influence allow for future conversations about other topics that might make a real difference in their lives? I feel pretty confident that's a yes.

Understanding is the number one key to influence. Dr. Stephen Covey calls this Empathetic Communication or Empathetic Listening. The goal is to enter the other person's frame of reference. Or to put yourself in their shoes, as my dad used to say. That can happen through simple role play when you put yourself into the character you are playing. Knowing some of their backstory, their life experiences, and the perspectives that they formed due to those experiences, we gain an advantage. We begin to understand. Making the effort to do that role reversal, their perspective sounds less foreign. We can see how they came to embrace that perspective, understand their why, de-villainize them, and start to build some trust that could form a bridge for future influence in their lives. And them in ours!

When we filter what others say through our story, we can't understand theirs. We judge through the wrong filter and assume we know what they mean because we know what we would mean. For a silly example, you may hear someone say, "She is such a diva!" Automatically you think she is speaking negatively when, depending on your story, it could be a compliment. Maybe you are at a birthday party, and you politely decline the cake offered. Others may assume you are trying to lose weight when you may be allergic to gluten or diabetic. On a deeper note, let's say a new acquaintance shares that she has recently been through a divorce. If you have experienced divorce as well you may assume her heart is broken, because yours was, and respond in a way that doesn't connect with where she is at all. She may have been shut down for years, ruled by fear in an abusive relationship that dictated what she thought, did, and didn't do. She finally escaped and found a new freedom in getting to know her own worth, strength, and desires,

> "Understanding is the number one key to influence."

so the heartbreak is only for the years she lost by being in that relationship. Not for the divorce. You get the picture. Judging other people's situations and perspectives through our lens is often faulty. Taking the time to listen for the purpose of understanding can make a world of difference, to them and to you.

The hardest hurdle to jump in this process is

getting over the false belief that if we understand someone's perspective, we *must agree* with them. The second hurdle to jump is the fear that if we understand someone's perspective, we *might agree* with them.

We don't like to be wrong, do we?

My friend Michael McIntyre says the three things that keep us from moving forward more than anything else are 1) the need to be right, 2) the need to be in control, and 3) the need to look good. If we can get over ourselves long enough to lay down those concerns, we can step into a much larger place of influence and joy.

"When we filter what others say through our story, we can't understand theirs."

Respectful, attentive listening often reciprocates with the same, even when we have opposing views. Honor breeds respect, and opposition is taken off guard. When we listen to understand people with whom we disagree, often the door is opened for them to listen to us, as well. Understanding, trust, and respect then become possible on both sides of the bridge.

There is a power that comes with listening.

7

O is for Own

OWN. LET'S LOOK at the meaning of that word before we move on. I especially like these two definitions from dictionary.com:

Own means "to acknowledge as one's own; recognize as having full claim, authority, power, dominion, etc." and "to totally defeat, gain control over, or dominate in a competition." Wow. That's powerful.

"O" stands for *"Own your journey and the biases that come with it."*

What are biases? They are our strongly held, preconceived feelings and opinions toward a person or thing. When we own our biases, we are recognizing and admitting to preconceived feelings and opinions which opens us up to exploring the truth or falsehood of those biases. If we don't own them, acknowledge them, we continue to operate on assumption. Owning them makes room for exploring them to see if they are truth. So again, I want to say...

Own your journey and the biases that come with them.

Why?

Because ownership impacts our conversations. We don't care or invest nearly as much into those things we do not own.

Own your journey. Own your biases. We are to acknowledge them as being fully and uniquely our own, and we are to have full authority over them, defeating, gaining control over, and dominating anything related to them that would try to defeat us.

Life experiences make up our journey.

The stories we tell ourselves about those experiences create our biases.

When we own both our journey and biases, we can shift the trajectory of our journey and take authority over negative biases, totally defeating and gaining control over them. We can demolish the negative biases that have served us poorly, harming relationships and decreasing our influence.

Our experiences shape our journeys, for better

or for worse. The good news is we don't have to stay on the same journey we have been on because we own it. We can do with it what we choose. We can intentionally stop getting on the wrong roads.

> "Life experiences make up our journey. The stories we tell ourselves about those experiences create our biases."

The greatest thing about our journey is that it's not over. We can see it up to this very moment, but it will continue for every next second that we are alive. What will we do with that? How will we use the rest of our journey to make a difference, to help others, and to be the best of all God made us to be?

Blame and shame are common travel companions, but blaming others and shaming ourselves only leaves us powerless. Blame and shame influence our conversations through accusation and depression, lacking empathy and creativity. It's time to take authority back over our life experiences—yes, even those that were done *to* us—and disallow those negative effects to dominate us anymore.

Our journey and our biases flow together more than we realize, with our biases sometimes directing our journey. We are going to explore this through experiences from my journey which I believe will be easily relatable to your own.

OWNING OUR JOURNEY AND BIASES

How do you own your journey? Imagine an aerial view of your life story, one you are observing instead of personally living. Doing this lets you see events from a vantage point that eliminates emotional binoculars. Nothing is magnified or reduced unrealistically.

Recognize the joyful parts and the painful ones. Looking from that aerial view, objectively, we can see it all. We can then accept responsibility for where we are right now because of those experiences.

Objectivity separates us from some of the emotions involved in our journey, allowing us to see our life events more clearly. It doesn't discount the emotion; it just lessens the ability those emotions have to cloud our vision. We can see, without being immersed in, the emotional aspects of our journey's impact.

My experiences are different from yours and yours are different from everyone else. I have learned great lessons from others, and have applied them to my personal journey, gaining much benefit. My hope is that you can do the same and apply the lessons I have learned to your journey as well.

Years ago, I had a traumatic memory emerge from my childhood. It was late at night and all my household was asleep except for me. I was journaling, which I habitually do, when a memory from decades before surfaced. It was a slow rise to the surface, like opening a photo album in slow motion and only seeing the bottom corner of the page, then a little higher up, then more towards the center, until the entire picture was laid open in full view. It wasn't shocking, which still surprises me. But it was scary, as if I felt what I felt back when I was in that situation. It also made me very angry. And sad. I knew that the "younger me" had been scarred deeply and affected in ways that I was only waking up to that very night.

I don't know how long I sat there, tears flowing, as I just whispered, over and over, *"Oh God. Oh, God. How did I not remember that?"*

As hard as that night was, I needed to get that portion of my journey back. I didn't need to remember for the sake of remembering. I needed to remember so that I could understand how the emotions lodged somewhere under the surface were impacting me, and how they had for years. Recognizing and remembering the helplessness I felt, the vow to never be vulnerable again, the behavior that the vow required, the fear, the anger, the grief. I needed to remember all of that. I needed awareness of its effects on my physical body as well as my emotions. Now that I am aware, I can own those effects. I can take responsibility for those things being a real part of my journey. I can break that vow and choose to not let it or any other thing dominate my emotions and behavior anymore. You can do the same.

About a year after that memory came to the forefront, I began having one discovery after another. I got a much broader picture of what had been a part of me all along. I discovered *why* I have had certain feelings, tendencies, and behaviors. Understanding that *why* opened a new way to view the experiences. Instead of getting stuck in the emotion, I was encouraged by it because I now had clarity on *why* I felt like I did. The *why* is important, and the most valuable takeaways came from my understanding the following things about myself:

- I was in certain environments long enough as a child to learn it wasn't safe to show vulnerability, so I focused on being strong which required a denial of any weakness.
- I grew up learning to discern who had the power in almost every situation and then determined whether that person was a friend or enemy. There was no neutral ground.
- As an adult I often had a hard time seeing

my limitations because I subconsciously denied my weaknesses. (That was both a blessing and a curse.)

- Loyalty, justice, and directness were greatly valued.
- I was highly independent.
- I loved challenges.
- I felt anger easily although I had gotten more diplomatic in the display of it.

Understanding life's impact on me provided many aha! moments. They exposed my strongest bias repeatedly.

Aha! I took the challenge because I wanted to prove I am strong. (Bias that vulnerability is bad.)

Aha! I can hardly walk this morning because I refused to admit my limitations at the gym yesterday. (Bias that weakness is bad.)

Aha! I spoke in an overly direct manner because I pegged the person as an enemy and couldn't show any weakness. (Bias that strength always has the upper hand.)

Do you see a theme here?

That all hits home with me like a boat in the water or a nest in a tree. You know what I mean? It just fits where I lived much of my life. The thing is, when a storm comes it can capsize boats and blow nests out of trees. Meaning a good fit for calm weather may not be a good fit for storms. Hard conversations are in the storm category. In order to navigate them well, we need to step away from what *feels* right and step into what *is* right. In hard conversations, vulnerability usually wins. Since weakness is a sign of our humanity, it is relatable and appreciated. Strength might actually lose the upper hand.

What feels like a good fit might be dangerous, or at least counterproductive. Those conversations that need to be had with courage, humility, authenticity, integrity, and respect don't do well with people who refuse vulnerability. Relationships need vulnerability. They need honesty, and nobody is always strong. Pretending otherwise is dishonest.

Understanding the impact life has had on us provides us with some aha! moments. Those aha! moments reveal our biases, and our biases often work against the very things we think we are working toward.

Connecting repeated behaviors to underlying beliefs about life experiences builds a roadmap to the *why* behind our present-day feelings, tendencies, and behaviors. It all becomes clear. It can for you, too.

So, what do we do with that? To disconnect

from the behaviors that hold us back we need to convince our emotions that we aren't in those situations anymore. Depending on the level of trauma, that might require some type of therapy. Or it may just require a mind shift that acknowledges real situations have affected what we feel and do, but now we can use that understanding to remind ourselves those situations are no longer active. We aren't in those same situations anymore. We can let go of the not-so-beneficial behaviors and trade them in for what is needed today. For what is needed in the conversation or with the person right in front of us.

Awareness of what drove some old behaviors, feelings I didn't know I had because I hadn't allowed myself to feel them, helped me understand why I did what I did. It showed me the cause for my actions and reactions and freed me to let go. It gave me a framework to deconstruct the faulty structures I had built in my mind and heart. It helped my *why* change from a protective one to a courageous one. From a defensive *why* to an offensive one. I am not in the dark anymore. Old behaviors don't have to rule me. What an eye-opener!

I once thought I had walked through all the heart healing possible, but I now believe it's an ongoing process in this life if we allow it to be. And it is beautiful. I am thankful to God and now keenly aware of when independence or stubbornness or judgment begins to rise. More importantly, I understand *why* and self-correct when necessary.

Healing is necessary for a healthy *why*. It is also needed for healthy conversations. It is needed to deconstruct loud. Otherwise, we get triggered and respond from an experience we are no longer living in. One that doesn't even relate to what's happening today.

We have choices. We can either stay in the minutia, or we can move on. Get some help to move forward if necessary. This strong girl appreciates help more than ever. I finally realize admitting your vulnerabilities is one of the most courageous things anyone can do.

Hopefully, these experiences help you to see what you are looking for. You are looking for blind spots, stuffed emotions, and the events that caused them. You are also looking for the beauty in your journey and the life lessons from those as well.

"Admitting your vulnerabilities is one of the most courageous things you can do."

MORE ABOUT BIASES

It is so easy to see others' biases, and without serious intentionality, it can be near impossible to see ours. Let's explore more of how they are formed and why they tend to stick around.

As we have said, the stories we tell ourselves about our life experiences form these biases. They are often skewed thoughts, feelings, and opinions, although sometimes they are accurate. For the most part, they are hidden, but we can bring them to light. We can disconnect from them. They can be straightened out. That is important.

Skewed biases make for skewed conversations just like hidden emotions skew the understanding of our journeys. When we bring those biases into the light, we can evaluate them and shift what is needed so that our positive experiences increase.

Biases create beliefs, and those beliefs come directly from our assumptions about *why* we experienced what we did. Assumptions. Hear that? We take these beliefs on without proof, and usually with skewed truth. A prominent memory etched in my mind from junior high is a great example.

After my parents divorced, I moved with my mom to a new city and didn't have a lot of friends for a while. Over the summer months, a casual friendship with a girl who lived near me became a best-friendship, and we did pretty much everything together. Another girl I didn't know well sought me out and told me I should try out for cheerleader the following year at the junior high school I would be attending. She was a year older than me, and already a cheerleader at that school. She told me I could easily make cheerleader, I just needed to dump my best friend because people wouldn't vote for me if I hung around her. She wasn't "popular" enough. As I said, she didn't know me well. I told her what she could do with her suggestion in no uncertain terms.

Soon after, my best friend started distancing herself from me. I could tell something was wrong, but when I asked, she denied it. She stopped coming over, didn't answer the phone when I called, and didn't answer the door when I went to her home. I racked my brain trying to think of every possible scenario that could have caused her to be angry with me, but I couldn't think of a thing. School started. She wasn't speaking to me at all by this time, but I made new friends. School was fun overall, although I was sad about what had happened with my friend and confused about why. I was on the Student Council and enjoyed that, but I refused to try out for cheerleader. The bad taste was still in my mouth from that cheerleader's suggestion, and I didn't want to be in any part of her world.

Several months into my 7th-grade year, the sister of my former friend confronted me, telling me what a snake I was. That's when I found out the cheerleader had gone to my friend (after my adamant refusal to trash our friendship) and told quite a convincing lie. She told my friend I had come to her saying I wanted to try out for cheerleader but was concerned I wouldn't get votes if I was hanging out with my friend. Wow wow wow. And my friend believed her!

Being lied about isn't fun, but what hurts, even more, is when those you trust, those who know you best, those who should know you would never do such a thing, believe the lies. When the ones believing the lies are the very ones who should be disputing the lies. That's what hurts the worst.

That was my first, but not my last experience with people covering their butts by flipping the story. It was unfortunately also not my first or last experience with someone close to me believing the worst about me. Those are the worst kind of hurts, and it would be nice if all that ended in childhood, wouldn't it? Unfortunately, it doesn't. It is one of the uglier sides of humanity.

Due to many emotional betrayals, I have a loyalty bias. Loyalty is huge for me, and that looks like me believing the best in you, speaking only the best truth of you, and certainly not saying anything that would embarrass or negatively affect anyone's opinion of you. That is the conscious bias I live from toward others. I choose it. Because I never want my words, or lack of them, to be the cause of someone else experiencing pain.

What does that have to do with communication?

You can imagine how hard it would be for me to engage in a conversation where disloyalty is evident. When someone shares information that would embarrass someone else, information they said they wouldn't share, or personal information that is nobody else's business, those types of disloyal behaviors really rile me up. I need two things to stay in that conversation. First, I need awareness. Awareness that what they are saying is rubbing hard against my bias. Second, I need to quickly run through the CHAIR qualities to see if I should remain in the conversation.

Do I see results coming from this conversation that would be worth sticking it out (courage)?

Am I thinking of them more than myself (humility)?

Am I being real with them (authenticity)?

Am I operating with honest motives (integrity)?

Can I look at them, respecting who they are as a person (respect)?

And if I can't be confident and comfortable in my stance on each one, I need to take a break from that conversation.

I obviously have a strong loyalty bias. It mostly serves me well, but in negative conversations like that, where disloyalty is evident, I have to actively own that bias to even hear the point that is being made, if there is one. And when trust is gone, the conversation is, too. It is not possible for me to walk with those I don't trust. Sometimes it's not even possible to talk with them. The CHAIR helps me decide. Do I even want to pull up a CHAIR?

I have learned two important things about myself from these types of experiences. I have learned that I want to be a loyal person whether others are or not. And I have learned that trust is too precious to give to just anybody. My alignments are much more tried, tested, and intentional than they used to be.

Our journeys are a mix of hard times and joys, so I would be amiss to not share one of my beautiful experiences. Beautiful biases have been created from it as well.

As a young teen, I moved to a different city and made some good friends quickly. Despite the negative mindset toward cheerleaders a couple of years before, I was encouraged again to try out for cheerleader and made the team. At summer camp our goal was to win the "spirit stick" to bring back to the school. On the first day of the competition, we did great. No mess-ups. Perfect timing. Everything clicked. And our energy was off the charts. Imagine how shocked we were to find out we got zero points toward a spirit stick. We were very upset. Going over every action we could remember of that day we tried to figure out what could have possibly gone wrong. Finding no answers, the ugly green giant showed up and we began talking about the team who had gotten the most points. *They weren't even that good. We did better than they did! Almost everybody did better than they did! Did you see how their timing was off?* Thankfully our pettiness didn't get the best of us. We decided to watch that team closely the following day and see if we could learn anything they were doing right that we weren't doing. And you know what we saw? We saw that they cheered for every team that competed just as wholeheartedly as they cheered when they were competing. Guess who won the most points that day, too? Yep! The not-so-great team.

What I learned that week was that greatness isn't only about performance. Greatness is focused on helping others be great, too. It's focused on helping others believe they can do it. It's about instilling you-can-win convictions in the hearts of everybody. That lesson has stayed a powerful part of my journey. It was the first leadership lesson I ever learned that really stuck with me. The best leaders aren't afraid of competition but encourage it. I have a win-win bias, and I plan on keeping it.

KNOW YOUR BIASES

Because biases are often a skewed version of reality, the probability that unhealthy behavior can result from our biases is high. When recognized, we can straighten up the skewed places and have some healthy convictions as well. Those biases, in mostly healthy ways, show up for me like this:

If you have something to say about me, say it to my face.

When you make a mistake, own it.

You are only blaming to avoid shame.

Cheer for everyone; it may be the very thing that makes you a champion.

Some of them have a harsh tone, don't they? Even if the sentiment is right, when the tone is off, it is a red flag that something internally is off, too. I am aware of that. I can be hardcore sometimes. I am working on it, and thankful for the *awareness* that these are a few of the ways my feelings and opinions can get skewed toward relationships. It's not always pretty, but I am being honest with myself.

When we own these things, we see the impact in our conversations. But unexplored biases can provide a faulty lens through which we filter others' words, so when we recognize the bias and refuse to let it be our filter any longer, the ability to communicate with understanding and respect increases significantly. So does the ability to know the conversations we are not to enter.

I have shared a few of my observations and biases. I hope you will grab a big dose of courage and do the same for yourself. Own your journey. Observe it objectively. Then explore what biases may be showing up with you, perhaps still unaware.

8

U is for Understanding

IT DOES LITTLE good to listen to others if we don't try to understand them.

For people to feel heard, there must be some level of understanding or at least some sincere attempts at trying to understand. Feeling heard is important. It creates trust, and there is a high cost to low trust.

You can tell if a person genuinely wants to understand by listening to their responses. If they ask questions that show a willingness to hear other perspectives, they are probably genuinely trying to understand. If they ask questions that are leading the listener to a certain way of thinking, questions that sway the listener's response, they are probably not. And you can be sure they are not interested in understanding another perspective when they have

a comeback for everything said, or continually answer with a "But...." giving a counter opinion. That
doesn't mean it is wrong to have a counter opinion.
It is certainly not. It just means there is very little
engagement in the understanding process when
someone continually interjects their opinion while
someone else is sharing. And it's the same for those
who don't ask questions at all. We gain understanding by asking questions and getting answers. People
who never ask about you, how you are, what you
think about something, what you mean by something you said, etc... are not terribly interested in
understanding you.

What are we trying to understand?

We want to understand not only

1. *what* they are saying, but
2. *why* they feel strongly about it, and
3. *how* they came to gain their unique perspec-
    tive.

Understanding these things requires listening
for the stories behind the words. Those stories express the why. They uncover the marks that were
left on the lives of those who lived those unique experiences.

We all have marks on our lives. Physical, mental, emotional, spiritual, or relational. The experiences that only we have lived from our perspective
shape those marks. Without understanding how

others' marks shaped them, we simply assume. Usually the worst. Especially if we disagree with their views.

There are around eight billion people in this world, and each one has had unique experiences that determine their biases. Each one also lived through that experience with their own unique perspective and feelings about it. That's eight billion biases! I can't even wrap my brain around what that many biases look like. But what's even more crazy is that we don't try to. We just assume we know what somebody means by what they say because we filter it through our own biased lens, which is a skewed lens when it comes to others' experiences. Even if we have lived through similar circumstances, we can still only understand in part unless we ask and listen to the more they have to share. There is treasure in the more.

With each of our experiences being so completely unique, as well as the lessons we learn from them, it is no wonder there are so many misunderstandings and assumptions about what, why, and how we all think.

Intentionality is key. If we are to understand different perspectives, we must be intentional. We have not lived the experiences of a single other person on this planet. Not fully. So, the best way to be intentional about understanding is to first *listen at-*

tentively with a desire to understand. Secondly, when needed, *ask questions to clarify what is really being said.* If you only think you know, you probably don't.

Seeking to understand is not for the faint of heart. I lost friends in 2020 for trying to understand others with whom they disagreed...or judged. Not everyone wants to understand or even wants to believe they may not understand. This understanding journey is not embraced by ones who believe they know the motives of others' hearts and actions. Enough said.

This next section may be a little heavy. It can bring great understanding, though, just as it did for me. I want to address this topic because of the benefits I received that were far greater than any uncomfortableness. It drives home the truth of how we don't understand all we think we do. As you read, consider opening and extending your heart and mind to reach for understanding. I am not asking for agreement. Just understanding.

STEPPING INTO THE UNCOMFORTABLE

Understanding often requires stepping into areas where you are extremely uncomfortable. My year for that was 2020. What a year. That's a year all of us stepped into areas where we were extremely uncomfortable, but not of our own choosing. Of course, there was Covid. But I am thinking more of the racial tensions, much of which was stirred by the death of George Floyd.

Notice I didn't say they were *caused* by the death of Mr. Floyd. I said *stirred*. When things are stirred it shows they were already there. Maybe just under the surface. Maybe boiling on top. Whatever it looked like in your world at the time, the circumstances surrounding his death stirred pain and anger that was in the hearts of many people at different levels and for different reasons. Please be sensitive to that as I share with you how I dealt with what I didn't understand.

Some of you tensed up at the mention of Mr. Floyd's death. You may have remembered the video footage on every news outlet and social media platform. Some tensed up from remembering the aftermath of it. The riots. The protests. My guess is that many of you tensed up, though, because you wonder where I am going with this.

I want to ask you to please *listen to understand*. I assure you with my solemn promise there is no political motive behind it. As political as this horrible incident became, none of my experience is political. It is extremely personal. And the best way I know how to express it is to go back to a very raw blog post I wrote a few nights after Mr. Floyd's death. Here are a few excerpts from that post:

"Middle of the night. I can't breathe. Not in the same way George Floyd couldn't breathe. Mine is a can't get a deep breath kind of not being able to breathe. It is an immense-grief-in-the-midst-of-a-horrifying-reality-while-not-knowing-what-to-do kind of not being able to breathe. And words aren't enough, but I don't know what else to do. I can't even think straight."

"So here I am fumbling around in the dark asking WHY???"

"WHY do we hate? WHY do we hurt each other? WHY do we feel superior? WHY do we abuse and pervert power?"

"And I want to say I AM SORRY."

"Perhaps the closest way I can identify is in the fear of waiting and wondering and hoping and praying your child is safe. I know the monster in your gut that won't turn loose as you wait and hope and pray with everything in you that your child will just walk through the door. Safe. I know the fear that tortures you with thoughts that they may not. Night after night after week after month after year.

So, finding out that in George Floyd's last minutes, while being held down and completely powerless, he called out for his mama, brings this already devastating injustice to a whole different level inside of me."

"This is, admittedly, a feeble attempt to express

the heaviness and grief and horror and sorrow in my heart. But I invite constructive conversations that could produce positive actions, although I don't presume to know what those might look like."

"But this mama cares and I want to step across the uncomfortable dividing line and hear the things that will undoubtedly challenge me."

Those were the things in my heart. It was a heart dump and a lot of brain confusion. To be honest, a big part of me wondered if it was racial at all. It was horrible and unjust and cruel no matter what color your skin. But I am white, so that is easy for me to think. Where I finally landed was knowing that whether this specific incident was racial injustice or just outright injustice, it had certainly stirred up a lot of pain and anger from undealt with racial tensions...and I knew enough to know something besides politics was underneath that.

I decided to reach out to some of my black friends and associates to have some conversations I never knew needed to happen.

They were gracious. So very gracious to their white friend who was unaware of the racial issues many still deal with in this country. I grew up knowing that some people didn't like others because of their color, but I was also very confused by that. I didn't understand it. It didn't make sense. I really believed the little song we sang in church as children that said, "Jesus loves the little children. All the children of the world. Red and yellow, black and white, they are precious in His sight. Jesus loves the little children of the world." Call me naïve. I understand. But I did not know there was a problem that was bigger than a few scattered ignorant people. I never grew out of believing the words to that song. I am just being real.

In asking to have some uncomfortable conversations, I heard the life experiences of over a dozen people. I talked and asked questions and listened and tried to understand. The people I spoke with were a mix of political parties, faith backgrounds, and socio-economic statuses... but every single one had a similar story. Some grew up in "the hood" while others grew up in "white neighborhoods." What amazed me was that the stories didn't change. Every single one of them had stories of injustices because of their skin color. Injustices through stories passed down from generations before to the injustices their parents had experienced, to their own experiences, and even some that their children had experienced. It was a perspective adjustment for me for sure.

Then I heard about this crazy list. They just called it "the list." Say that to a black person, and they nod their head with an "Mmm hmm." They all know about the list. Say it to a white person and we say, "Huh? What do you mean? What list?" But each one of the people I spoke with had been conditioned by this list that told them how to act when approached by a white person that might have any kind of authority. They all knew to keep their hands out of their pockets and in plain sight, what tone to speak in, whether to make eye contact or not, to say "ma'am" and "sir" and the list goes on. Talk about a new understanding. I taught my children to say "ma'am" and "sir", too, but not for the same reasons. It wasn't for their safety. It was because it was polite. These friends' parents taught them "the list" as a rule of conduct to keep their babies safe.

My heart broke. I never knew.

I now understand. As much as I *can* understand without living their experiences, I understand. And I am so sorry.

Several of my friends have chosen to throw the list away. To stop living by an old code that should never have been. I want to celebrate that. It thrills my heart. They are choosing to walk a new way, even when it goes against their conditioning, even when it is scary, because they want to see a new way. To live a new way. I want that new way, too. I believe most of us do. We just need to understand, which often requires stepping into areas where we are extremely uncomfortable. But it is worth it.

YOU ARE NOT IN PHILADELPHIA ANYMORE

My husband, Mike, moved to Texas from Philadelphia when he was in 6th grade. At sporting events in Philadelphia, if your team was doing well, people yelled, "YAY!!!" If your team was not doing well, they yelled, "BOO!!!" When Mike first told me this, I cringed. I grew up in Texas! You don't boo your own team! Who does that? Evidently, Philadelphians do that. Mike did that. It was normal to him.

When football season rolled around, Mike was invited to a high school football game with a friend. The friend's father took them, and you guessed it! (Are you cringing? You must be Texan. Or at least from the South.)

Mike was excited. Sitting in the bleachers, a voice came over the loudspeaker asking everyone to stand for the National Anthem and the Pledge of Allegiance. Soon after, the game began.

Their team was doing great, and Mike was having so much fun! Standing and yelling, "YAY!!!" at the top of his lungs with every good play was exhilarating. But when the tide turned and they started fumbling the ball and missing passes, Mike, completely unaware of the people's reactions around him, was just as exhilarated standing and yelling, "BOO!!!" at the top of his lungs. It wasn't until weeks later that the friend told Mike his dad said he would never take Mike to a game again because of his rude behavior.

Friday night football is a big deal in Texas. In small-town Texas, it is a big deal for the whole town to show up for the high school games. People who lived in my small town were known as Harvesters. That was the high school mascot, and whether you ever went to that high school or not, if you lived in the town you were a Harvester. I was born there, and moved before going to the high school, but am still considered a Harvester. Football is a community event in these places. Supporting the team equals supporting the town. Booing the team showed support for neither.

Remember that "U" stands for "understanding the biases of others due to their unique experiences." Unfortunately, that father didn't take the time to understand Mike's prior experiences. He just assumed he was a rude kid. If he had asked why he was yelling "boo," or pointed out that others weren't, Mike could have realized the wrong message he was sending and stopped. That father could have gotten to know a really great kid, too, if he had taken the time.

REMEMBERING

Remembering the *need* to understand others' stories is probably a greater issue than understanding the stories themselves. We need to remember *we* have a need, instead of assuming *they* have a problem.

When behavior is subconscious, and our assumptions often are, then the behavior becomes a habit and it takes some form of action on our part to change that. We have to see what we haven't seen before to realize the need to do things differently.

Going through life with blind spots is not how I want to live life. I got very intentional in 2020 about listening to every conversation with ears to hear the more that isn't being said. When I sense there is more, or don't understand their why, I ask questions. The answers dispel my assumptions and show the person I really care. Trust is built and doors are opened for future conversations to have some kind of influence or go deeper. It's a wonderful thing.

Life is too short to fall into judgment over and over because of blind spots. Open your eyes to see the more, or to at least ask for the more. You will discover relationship-building and the ability to positively influence others at a whole new, genuinely authentic level.

What action will you take to remember there is a need to understand beyond what you see?

9

D is for Develop

D STANDS FOR "Develop new ways to move forward."

What an amazing realization that we don't have to keep doing the same thing over and over. We can Listen to others, Own our own biases as we are listening to be sure we don't filter their words through our experiences, Understand their biases by asking questions to get a broader perspective of the experiences that helped shape their perspectives/opinions/convictions, and then Develop new ways to move forward based on what we have discovered.

Innovation and creativity are given free rein in a judgment-free zone, and that is what we create when we follow the L.O.U.D. process.

In the last chapter, I told you a story about my

husband, Mike, who moved to Texas from Philadelphia as an elementary school student and hadn't yet learned Texas etiquette for sporting events. What's crazy to me in that whole scenario is that the father passive-aggressively allowed the behavior throughout the entire game, and then imposed consequences of which he still didn't communicate. Instead, his son had to tell Mike weeks later. Passive aggression is a loud behavior. Both Mike and his friend felt the effects of it. Mike never went to a game with his friend's family again. That's sad.

That is what happens when we don't listen, own, and understand. There is no foundation for developing new ways to move forward.

Suppose the father would have corrected Mike. Told him to stop. That would have at least been a clue to Mike that something was off with his behavior, even if he wasn't sure what. It would have been even better if the father had *asked* Mike about his behavior. Like...*What would your parents think about you behaving like this?* Mike would have then had a chance to explain that they were the ones who showed him the behavior, which would ultimately have led to them both understanding that what was normal in Philly wasn't normal in Texas. A new way to move forward would have developed based on both of their discoveries.

Past generations don't own a patent on that behavior. We see it all the time, even with no children involved. Adults are less mature in their speech than I have ever known. Cancel culture and judgment justice are rampant.

Thankfully there were many open and honest conversations when I was trying to sort out the racial issues I finally saw in 2020. The conversations opened my eyes and heart to experiences I hadn't lived. They affected me deeply because of the deep wounds in the hearts of those I loved as well as the hearts of those they loved whom I will never know. Respectful communication was the bridge that provided safety on both sides of the conversation. Both sides of the understanding. Change happens with respectful communication.

Understanding what my friends and their families experienced, even in the day-to-day routines like going to the store and pumping gas, I knew there was an issue I needed to put my attention toward. Something was being un-

"Innovation and creativity are given free rein in a judgment-free zone."

covered for me. Something I hadn't seen before, and it felt important on a level that was weighty. I had some responsibility for what I discovered. Since then, I have become both more sensitive and more fierce in my love, protection, and understanding toward others.

Do I live out my convictions like you do? Probably not. Likely I am either too something or not enough of something else. I can't let either judgment stop me from moving forward in the way I feel strongly convicted, though. Something was uncovered that affected me deeply, and I am different because of it in my interactions with others.

One relationship at a time, change is happening. Change won't happen by a miracle wand being waved over the world, although that might sound nice to some. Change, to a great degree, will come when each of us chooses to begin personally embracing and acting on the convictions in our hearts to facilitate the change we hope to see in this world. Consistent, persistent action brings change. One person, one relationship, at a time.

Whether the issues you face involve family members, co-workers, community issues, church discord, or the politics involved in all of them, you have choices to make, and your choices determine whether things will stay the same or change. One person taking a stand and doing things differently makes a difference, just like one rock thrown in a pond makes ripples that reach the other side. Nobody taking a stand, just like nobody throwing a rock, keeps the pond still and stagnant.

What difficulties are you facing?

What challenges keep you awake at night?

What relationships need repair?

When you listen to others, own your biases, and understand others' biases, you can develop new ways to move forward. Together.

WHERE DO WE GO FROM HERE?

It doesn't do any good to just *know* the process. It's kind of like church. It doesn't do any good to just *know* what God says. The rubber meets the road when we choose to apply that knowledge and turn it into action. How many people sit for years, listening to their favorite preacher, conference speaker, or business leader, only receiving more knowledge they don't apply?

I desire transformation. In myself, in others, and in our relationships with God and each other. So where do we go from here?

PART THREE is full of opportunities for you to explore what this process could look like for you and your relationships. It includes:

- Reflection Exercises from Part One
- Reflection Exercises from Part Two

- Two checkups designed to help you determine your personal, relational, character,
and action needs
- An opportunity to Jump In and start the
process

All the exercises are designed to help you gain
understanding and wisdom for moving forward in
your own unique circumstances and relationships.

10
REFLECTION EXERCISES

THERE ARE NO right and wrong answers to these questions. My hope is that you will take your time to explore them, think deeply about them, and answer with complete honesty. This can be done alone or in a group, whichever you believe would be most beneficial, authentic, and challenging. It can be in a day, over weeks, or even months. The benefit comes from being crystal clear, however long that takes.

Questions are divided into the same sections as the book in case you want to look back over any notes or underlining you did to refresh your memory. You will get the most out of each section if you will take the time for a quick review.

Have fun!

Be honest!

Transform...yourself, your relationships, and your influence.

REFLECTION EXERCISES

FROM PART ONE: WHAT IT IS

THE MEANING OF LOUD:

1. How have you displayed loud behavior?
2. How do you respond to others' loud behavior?

DISCOVERING A DIFFERENT WAY:

1. How have you witnessed the power of respect?
2. What fears come to mind in regard to relational conflict?
3. Do you tend to shrink back or attack?
4. In what ways have you worked against the very things you want the most?
5. How committed are you to discovering a different way?

DINNER LESSONS:

1. What are your thoughts about building respectful connections that foster trust despite differences?

2. Who comes to mind that you can potentially build a bridge to?
3. How will you do that?
4. Who needs you to listen so that they can be understood?
5. Who do you want to listen to you?
6. How can you open the door for those conversations to happen?
7. What mindsets are you aware you have that need to be changed?
8. What will be your first step forward?

PULL UP A CHAIR:

Looking at the CHAIR acrostic, where do you need to get gut honest with yourself and make some adjustments in each of these areas?

Courage:
Humility:
Authenticity:
Integrity:
Respect:

DECONSTRUCTING LOUD:

1. What constructs are you aware of that need to be deconstructed?
2. How will you take steps to do that?
3. What are some ways, whether in volume

or attitude, that you have seen "loud" constructed into your ways of communicating?

4. What steps will you take to dismantle your
loud?

REFLECTION EXERCISES

FROM PART TWO: HOW IT WORKS

L - LISTEN:

1. How well do you do with listening to those whose views oppose yours?
2. What stops you from listening?
3. How have you influenced or been influenced by manipulation?
4. How did it feel?
5. What were the results?
6. How have you influenced or been influenced by authenticity?
7. How did it feel?
8. What were the results?
9. How do you feel about the statement, "Understanding doesn't equal agreement"?

How do these three things keep you from moving forward:

- The need to be right
- The need to be in control
- The need to look good

O - OWN

This section requires some reflection before answering the questions. I suggest getting quiet in a place without distractions and glancing over your life journey beginning from an early age, then moving forward to today. Make notes about experiences that affected you, both positively and negatively. Nothing is silly. Nothing is too small. If it had an impact on you that you still remember, it is important. These are the things that will give you some aha! moments about the biases you hold.

1. What is one part of your journey you can observe objectively and own the influence it still has over you today?
2. What are two or more biases you recognize from experiences you have lived?
3. Are there places of grief you have left unhealed?
4. Are you aware of why you have certain not-so-beneficial behaviors?
5. Do you understand why other's behaviors sometimes affect your emotions so deeply?
6. What positive experiences have you learned from?

U - UNDERSTAND:

1. Is there someone that comes to mind whom you might have judged wrongly by filtering their words or actions through your own lens?
2. How can you be intentional to understand the story behind their words or actions?

If nobody specifically comes to mind, they will. Think now about how you can intentionally prepare to find out more about their story so that your perspective and understanding are broadened.

D - DEVELOP:

When you listen to others, own your biases, and understand others' biases, you can develop new ways to move forward.

1. What difficulties are you facing?
2. What challenges keep you awake at night?
3. What relationships need repair?

Where in your life and relationships do you need to develop new ways to move forward?

RELATIONSHIP CHECK

Think of family members and those closest to you. List them separately by name in a private journal or notebook, then answer these questions for each person:

1. What interests do we share?
2. What values do we share?
3. What values do we not agree on?
4. Are there any issues that have been stuffed or are smoldering?
5. Are there any new issues that need to be addressed?
6. Based on your answers, do you see some ways to strengthen your relationship?
7. For example, inviting them to do something you both enjoy?
8. Focusing on things that mean a lot to both of you?
9. Maybe speaking to them about something that has been under the surface for too long and may be putting tension on the relationship?

10. If the last one is the case, are you willing to engage them in a conversation that could bring resolution?

If so, remember to prepare yourself with the CHAIR exercise (the exercises for it are a few pages over), then use the L.O.U.D. process and start by asking them questions and really listening to understand. Don't filter what they say through your lens. Determine to understand why they feel the way they do! Review the four steps in Part Two to get clarity.

THEN...

Think of business associates, employees, or co-workers. List them separately in a journal or notebook and answer these questions about them:

1. Do I appreciate them?
2. Do I show them I appreciate them?
3. How do I show them?
4. How can I show them?
5. Do I have an issue with them that I haven't shared?
6. Do I sense they have an issue with me?
7. If so, how can I address that?
8. Based on your answers, what are some ways you can take action to strengthen your working relationship and let them know you appreciate them?

If a conversation is needed to address any issues, remember the L.O.U.D. process. Ask questions, listen to understand, listen for the story behind the words, and do all you can to understand. Reviewing the four steps of L.O.U.D. in Part Two of this book will help get you ready, but remember to always prepare with CHAIR exercises before entering a L.O.U.D. discussion.

CHAIR CHECK

Nobody can enter a successful L.O.U.D. discussion process without being sure they can pull up a CHAIR with confidence.

This section is designed for evaluation.

First, evaluate whether you are committed to having the conversation, because...

Not all conversations are worth having.

There. I said it. It's true.

Without a reciprocal desire to understand, we either step into a battle of the wills or one person does all the listening while the other does all the talking. Neither is productive, and both can leave relationships damaged.

Evaluate your commitment level, and if you *are* committed to having the conversation, the second evaluation involves being sure you can settle yourself into each of these five characteristics involved in pulling up a CHAIR.

In other words, are you willing to enter the conversation with **Courage, Humility, Authenticity, Integrity,** and **Respect**? For most conversations, I can answer "yes." To be gut honest, though, there are a few where I am not willing. Either I don't yet have the courage, humility, respect, or something. Something is lacking that is needed to set the conversation up for success. And I am not willing to enter a conversation set up for failure. Relationships are worth far more than taking that kind of a chance. When you can answer a gut honest "yes" to having all five CHAIR qualities, you are ready to have that conversation.

Assuming you are committed, here is the CHAIR Checkup:

COURAGE

Have you taken the time to determine what is more important than the fear of addressing the issue?

Define what is more important than that fear or apprehension.

Once you do that, determine whether you can keep your focus on that, even if the conversation goes in a direction you were not expecting, becomes uncomfortable, or has high emotion.

HUMILITY

Remember this doesn't mean thinking less of yourself, it means thinking of yourself less. Meaning simply that it is not all about you. Think of yourself less as you go into the conversation. Sure you have needs. I am not suggesting you ignore them. I'm just suggesting you table them until you have taken a genuinely humble approach to see what the other person thinks and feels first.

Are you willing to think of your opinions and perspectives less than you want to understand theirs?

AUTHENTICITY

None of this is any good without authenticity. If you are doing what you are doing so that you can get what you want, stop now. That's manipulation. But if you authentically want to listen so that you can more fully understand their thoughts and emotions and move forward together with new ideas and ways, then keep going.

What are your motives for listening?

INTEGRITY

If the person with whom you are planning to have this conversation knew what you know about your motivations for the conversation, would they trust you?

Better yet, if you knew someone else wanted to have a conversation with you because of the same motives you want to speak to the person you have in mind now, *would you trust you?*

Operating with integrity requires checking our motives to be certain they are trustworthy. Ask yourself WHY you are doing, saying, and planning the things you are.

RESPECT

Some of the biggest manipulators show respect to get what they want. Showing respect must be backed up by truly valuing respect, operating in respect, and refusing to disrespect, despite differences. One of the greatest attributes of respect is the honor it places even on those with different perspectives.

Where do you stand in this area?

Can you value a person who opposes what you stand for?

We can only do this when we get our eyes off the issue and on the person. We don't have to respect what others believe in. We just need to respect the fact that:

1. they are a person with unique experiences that influenced their convictions, and
2. they have a right to believe whatever they choose.

We don't have to agree.

Once you have completed this checkup, feel good about your answers, and are committed to operating in each quality throughout the conversation, you are ready to have a successful, productive, trust-building conversation that can strengthen your relationship and increase the impact of your influence. Congratulations!

Invite them to pull up a chair. Do it soon. Sitting on something that is uncomfortable for too long causes us to backpedal and second-guess our decisions. If you know it's right, just jump in!

JUMP IN

Mel Robbins is the author of a book called *The 5 Second Rule*. It addresses procrastination from a perspective I hadn't heard of until Robbins' voice was brought to my attention a few years back. She believes procrastination is a coping mechanism for dealing with stress, rather than a form of laziness which is how we often associate procrastination. Her solution is to replace feelings with action, instead of trying to replace feelings with different feelings. *The 5 Second Rule* is all about taking immediate action that ignores feelings and forces us to take the action we have been avoiding.

I place a high value on feelings and how they affect us. They affect our physical, mental, emotional, and relational health, so please don't think I am suggesting you ignore your feelings altogether. What I am suggesting is that *everything* is not about feelings. I am suggesting we not let our feelings be our decision makers. Like washing the dishes or taking out the trash or exercising or eating healthy. How we feel about those things has absolutely nothing to do with whether we should do them. We may choose not to do them because we don't feel like it, but in doing so we are elevating our feelings to a place of power that affects us negatively.

Emotions become important in decision-making processes when our own emotional well-being, or the emotional well-being of others is at stake. Decisions involving relationships often require a lot of emotional processing. What we choose to do or not do with certain people often depends upon the type of relationship we have with them and how the emotions related to that relationship impacts us mentally, physically, and emotionally.

For a simplified example, imagine you are invited to a movie you have been excited to see by a person with whom you have continual negative experiences. I would hope the negativity that comes with being around them would be enough to decline the invitation. However, if you are invited to the same movie with an encouraging, supportive friend, go and enjoy! Feelings play a role in almost everything involving relationships. That doesn't mean they should dictate the relationships, but they do play significant roles in the health of them.

Emotions positively impact us when we are working through emotional pain, seeking greater awareness of negative emotional triggers, or pretty much anything involving the need for compassion or forgiveness. However, emotions impact us negatively when we allow them to be the decision-makers for tasks that don't involve the emotional aspect of our being.

Whether encouraging, controlling, peaceful, fun, or abusive...relationships require emotional processing. You have likely done a lot of that processing in the Reflection Exercises.

In relationships, especially close ones, it is healthy to express our emotions to one another. This isn't about that. This is about times like you just got to in our last section when you are committed to an action that may be uncomfortable and need to prepare your heart and mind to go after it. This is a great time to embrace the 5 second rule.

The longer you sit and think about when, how, where, and why you are going to initiate that hard conversation, the more time your feelings have to activate a negative response. Sometimes you just have to do it. And when you have put in the work through these questions, you know if this is one of those times. You know if you are ready to initiate that hard conversation or not.

If you ended the CHAIR Checkup section knowing who you need to talk to and went through the heart/mind preparedness steps of each of the five characteristics, you are ready. So as Mel would say, count backward from five and when you get to one, be actively engaged in doing what you know you need to do. Pick up the phone, send a text, shoot over an email, or whatever is needed to get that conversation scheduled.

The only way to start is to start. Otherwise, we can think ourselves out of a great decision. Take the next step. Whether that step is to review the LOUD process, evaluate the CHAIR acrostic, or determine which relationship you need to start with. Whatever that next step looks like, it is time to get started.

Take that step!

BRENDA COX HARKINS is an author, speaker, mediator, professional life coach, and founder of Harkins Leadership Group. Brenda's passion for mining gold in people and building bridges for better relationships is shared with a love for her family, faith, good friends, good coffee, and west Texas sunsets. She and her husband Mike live in Texas, and feel so blessed to have their children and grandchildren live nearby.

You can connect with Brenda at:
brenda@brendaharkins.com.

Or follow her on Facebook, Instagram, or LinkedIn:
@brendacoxharkins

Or Twitter:
@brendaharkins

ACKNOWLEDGEMENTS

Since the beginning of 2022 I have filtered every major decision through this question:

Is it tightly and rightly aligned with my vision and mission?

Every person on this page is a significant part of that alignment. I am forever grateful.

Thank you first to my husband, Michael, who has encouraged, supported, prayed for, and believed in me and all my dreams for over 28 years. Your ability to listen to all my big ideas and break them down into smaller action steps is a gift that continues to move me forward and make straight paths through all my circles. I love you most.

Thank you to Janis McAdoo, my dear friend and marketing specialist, for your love and friendship and for putting order to my chaos for so many years...but especially as it relates to the LINAL project now. You are a treasure in so very many ways!

Thank you to Michael and Stacye McIntyre, Brianna McIntyre, and the Next Level Experience team for helping me get the clarity I needed to complete in 3 months what I had not been able to do in 7 years. You guys are amazing!

Thank you to Nick Poe, founder of Tall Pine Books, for listening to my ideas, for believing in and encouraging me to get the message of LINAL out, and for aligning with the beliefs that have compelled me to keep moving forward with this message. Your authenticity, humility, and generosity confirmed from the very beginning of this project that Tall Pine was a major part of staying tightly and rightly aligned.

Thank you also to Austin Penn and the rest of the Tall Pine Books team that have proofed, edited, and been more than patient with all my changes and revisions. You are awesome.

And finally, thank you to my publicist, Julie Nowacki, who is another essential part of this alignment. Julie, your heart for kingdom influence and the immediate spirit connection I felt with you have continued to bless me throughout this process. I look forward to all that is ahead working with you!